PIANO SOLO

MICHAEL GIACCHINO

SHEET MUSIC COLLECTION

Cover Photo by Andy Paradise

ISBN 978-1-70516-866-0

Visit Hal Leonard Online at
www.halleonard.com

World headquarters, contact:
Hal Leonard
7777 West Bluemound Road
Milwaukee, WI 53213
Email: info@halleonard.com

In Europe, contact:
Hal Leonard Europe Limited
1 Red Place
London, W1K 6PL
Email: info@halleonardeurope.com

In Australia, contact:
Hal Leonard Australia Pty. Ltd.
4 Lentara Court
Cheltenham, Victoria, 3192 Australia
Email: info@halleonard.com.au

CONTENTS

AS THE JURASSIC WORLD TURNS

from JURASSIC WORLD

Music by MICHAEL GIACCHINO

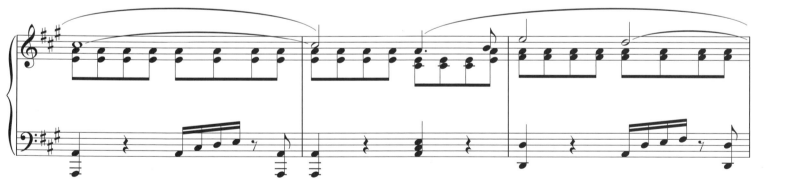

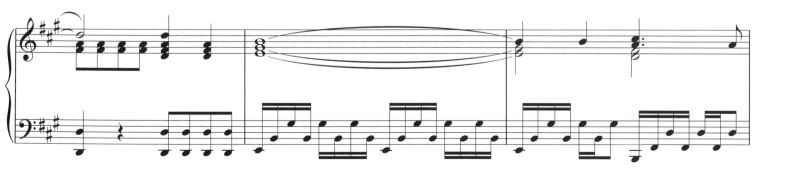

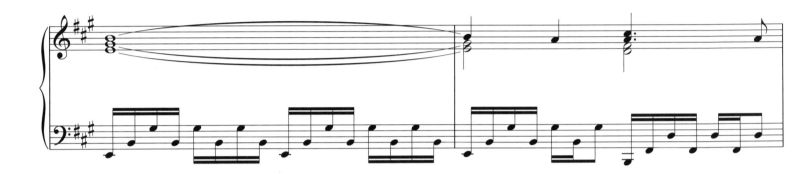

BUNDLE OF JOY

from INSIDE OUT

Music by MICHAEL GIACCHINO

Moderately fast

Moderately

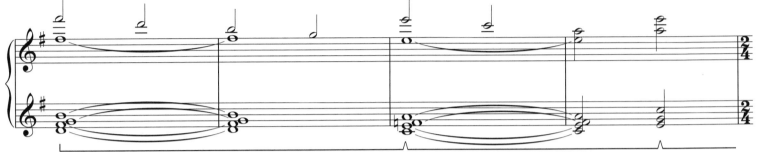

Moderately fast

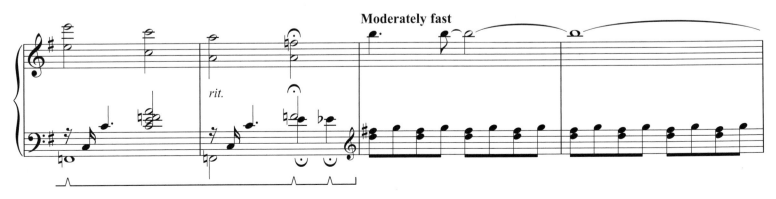

CROSSING THE MARIGOLD BRIDGE

from COCO

Music by MICHAEL GIACCHINO

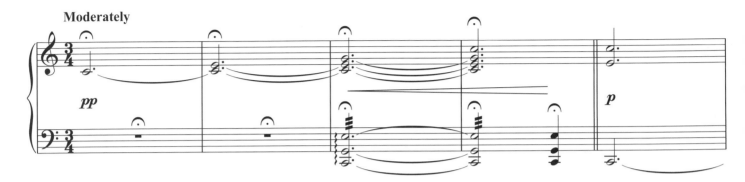

HERE COMES ELASTIGIRL – ELASTIGIRL'S THEME

from INCREDIBLES 2

Music and Lyrics by
MICHAEL GIACCHINO

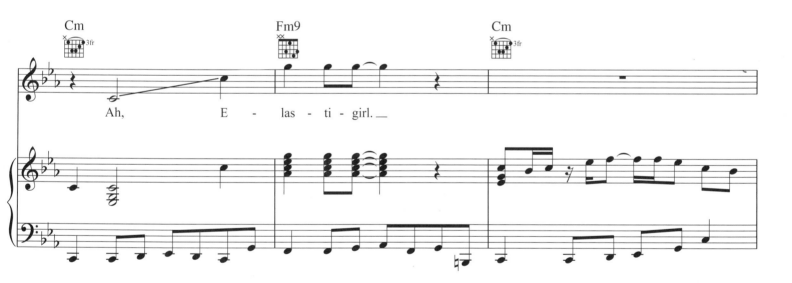

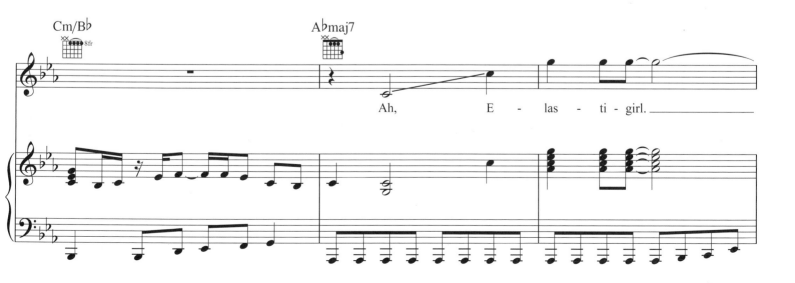

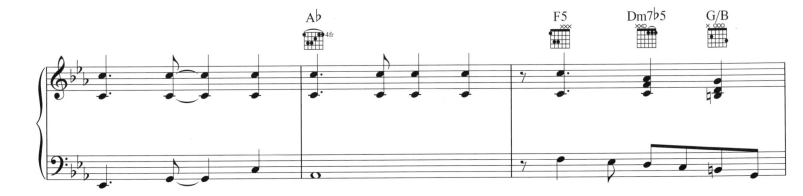

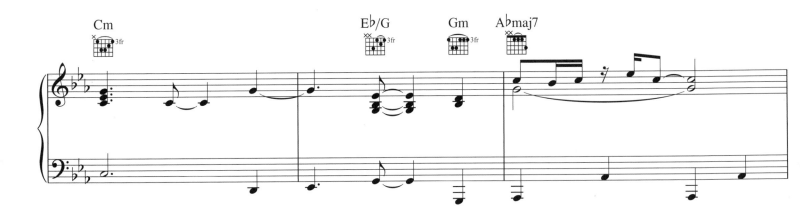

THE INCREDITS
from THE INCREDIBLES

Music by MICHAEL GIACCHINO

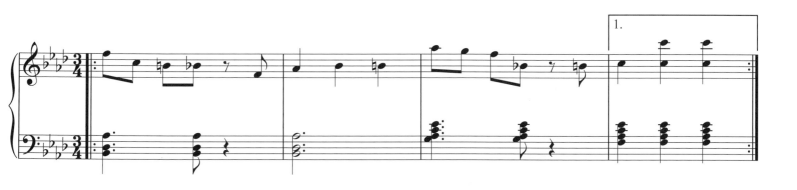

Sax solo ad lib.

JOHN CARTER OF MARS

from JOHN CARTER

Music by MICHAEL GIACCHINO

Moderately slow

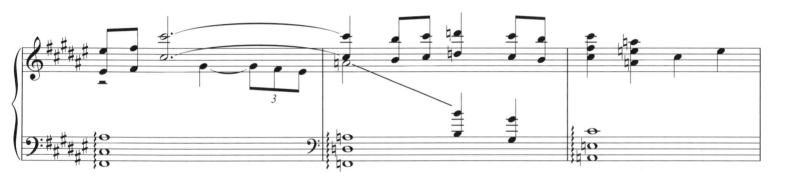

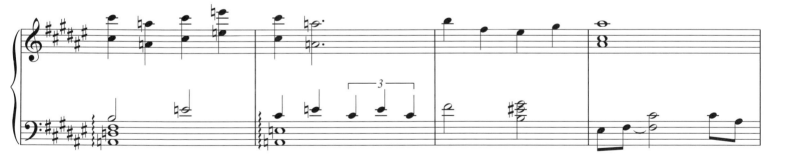

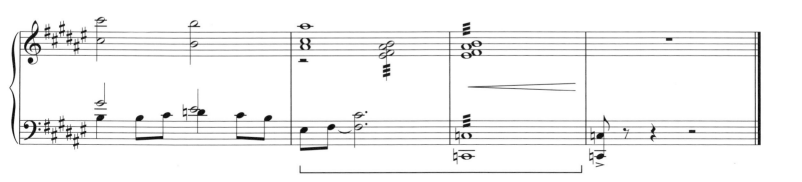

JUPITER ASCENDING – 3RD MOVEMENT

from JUPITER ASCENDING

Music by MICHAEL GIACCHINO

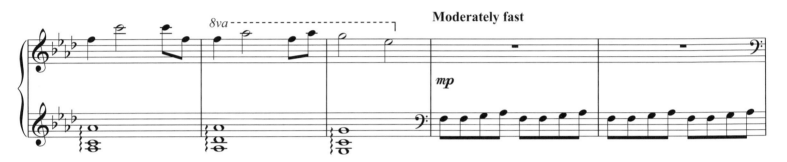

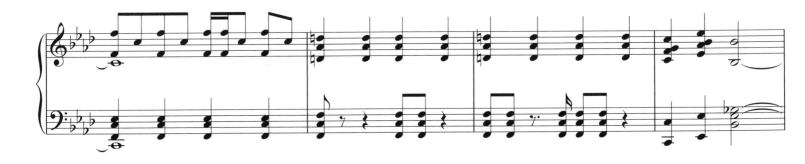

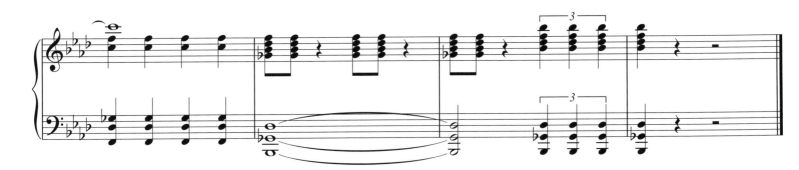

MASTER OF THE MYSTIC END CREDITS

from DOCTOR STRANGE

Music by MICHAEL GIACCHINO,
JEFFREY JAMES KRYKA and CHARLES LESLIE SCOTT

Moderately fast

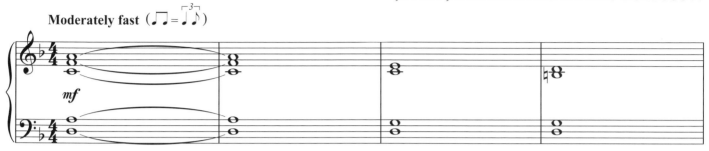

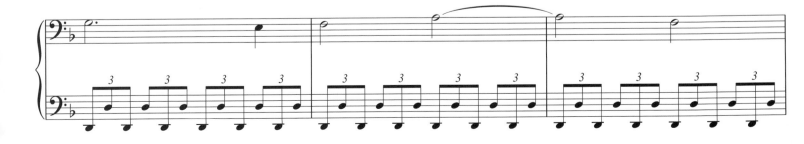

Slowly, freely

molto rit.

LIFE AND DEATH
from LOST

Music by MICHAEL GIACCHINO

Very slowly, freely

pp

Pedal ad lib. throughout

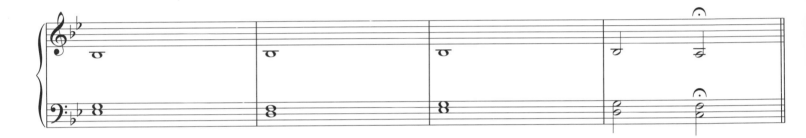

LIFE'S INCREDIBLE AGAIN
from THE INCREDIBLES

Music by MICHAEL GIACCHINO

LONDON CALLING
from STAR TREK INTO DARKNESS

Music by MICHAEL GIACCHINO

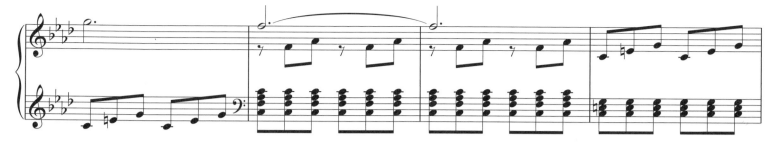

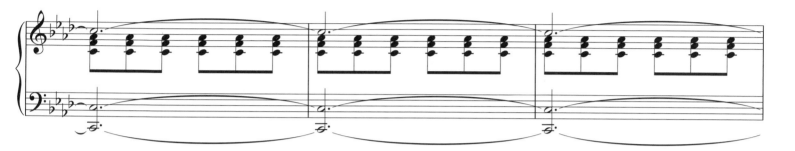

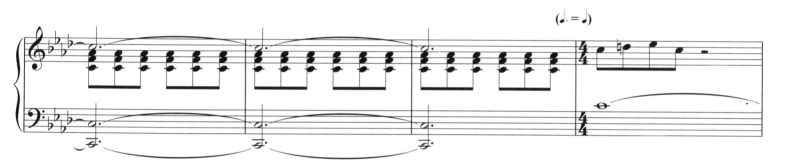

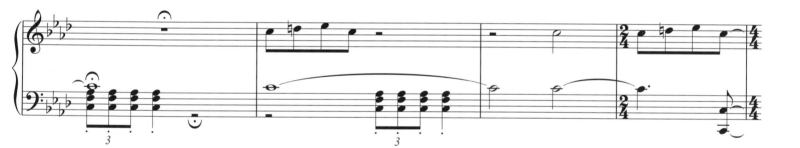

MARRIED LIFE

from UP

Music by MICHAEL GIACCHINO

Moderately fast

mp

With light pedal

cresc.

mf

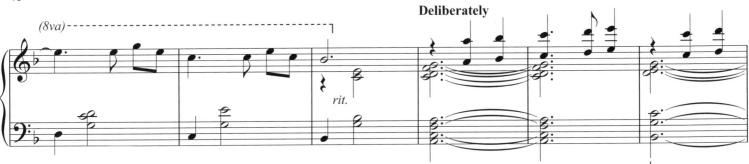

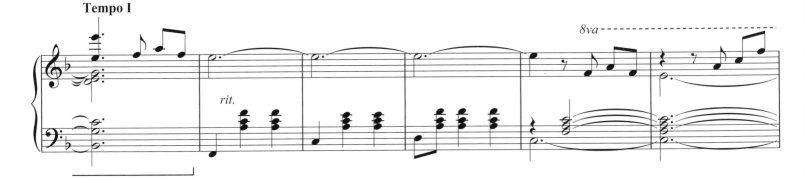

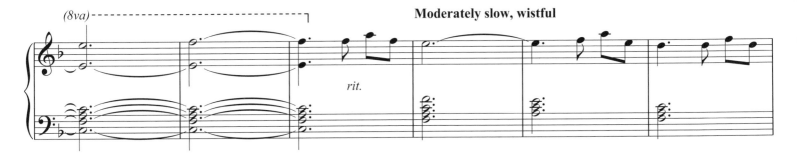

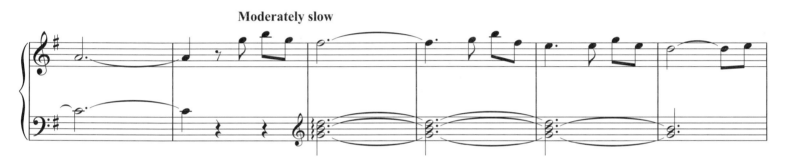

Moderately slow

MEDAL OF HONOR
(Main Theme)
from MEDAL OF HONOR

Music by MICHAEL GIACCHINO

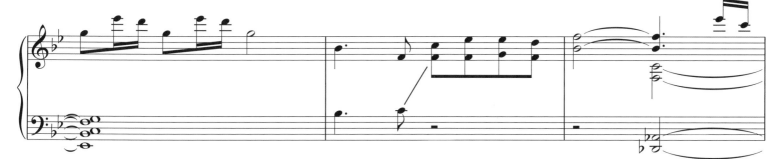

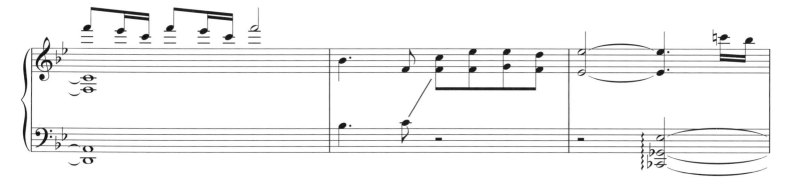

Faster

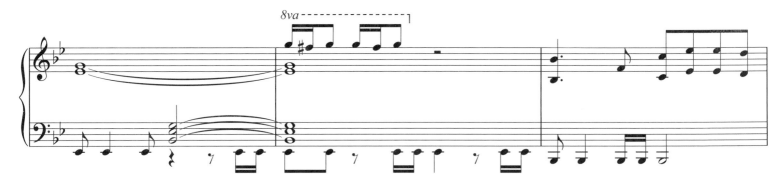

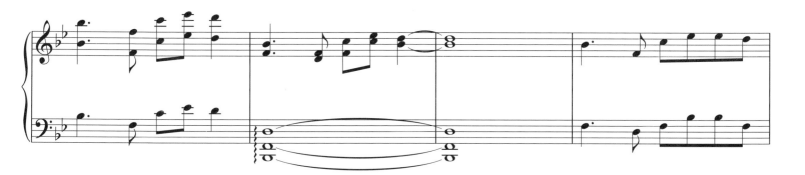

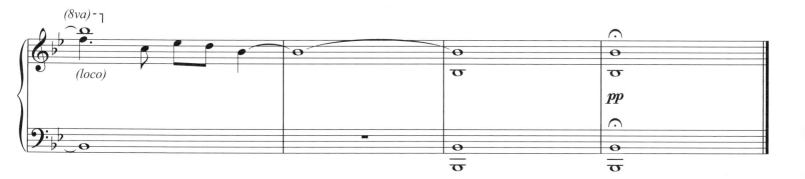

PARTING WORDS

from LOST

Music by MICHAEL GIACCHINO

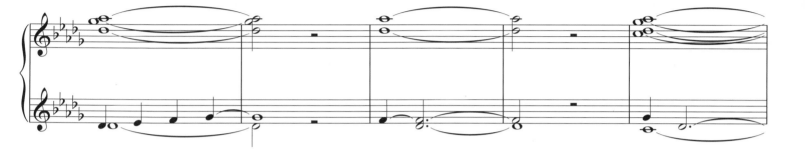

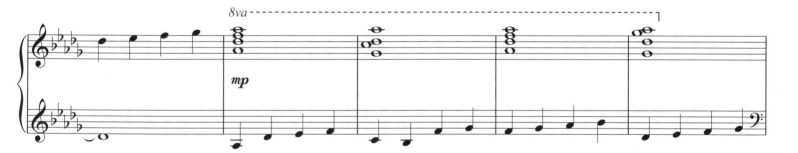

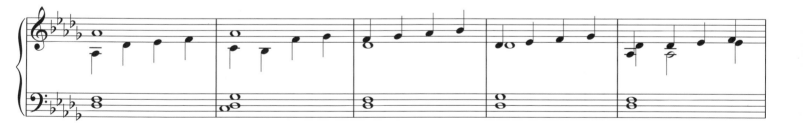

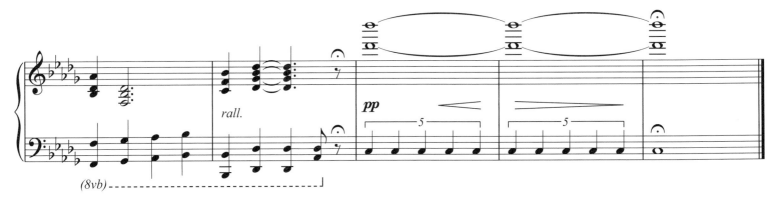

PIN-ULTIMATE EXPERIENCE

from TOMORROWLAND

Music by MICHAEL GIACCHINO

Moderately fast

With pedal

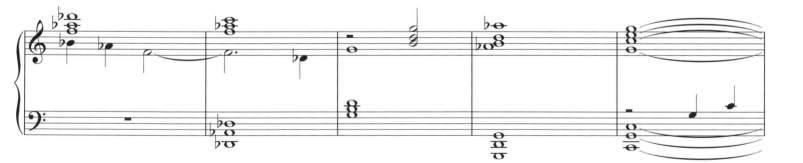

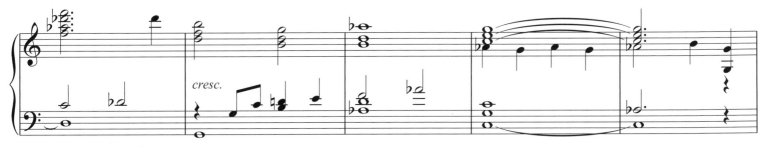

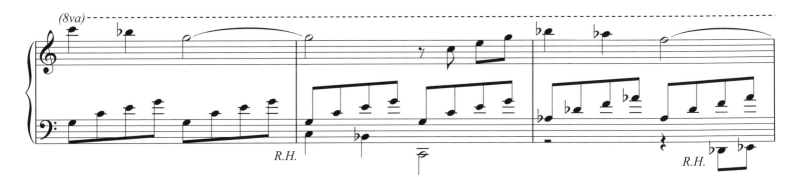

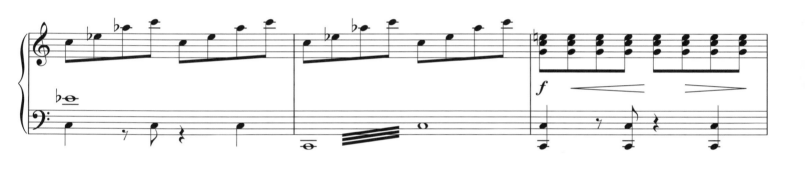

PLANET OF THE END CREDITS

from DAWN OF THE PLANET OF THE APES

Music by MICHAEL GIACCHINO

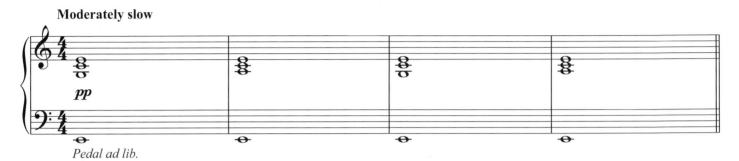

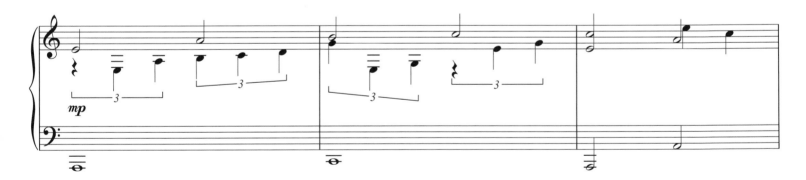

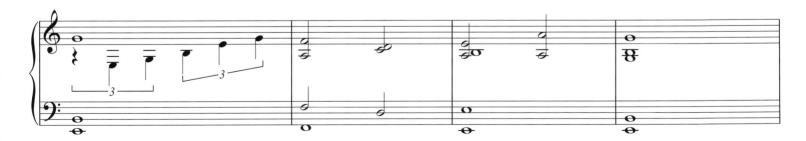

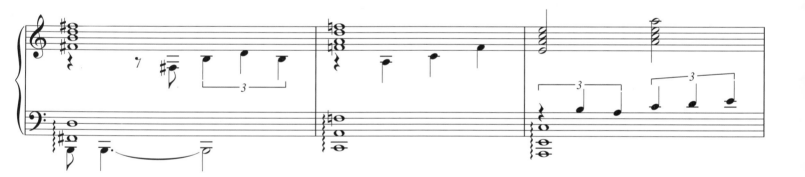

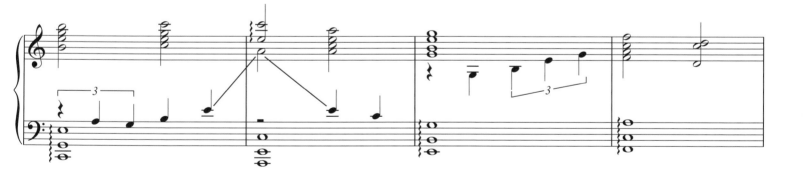

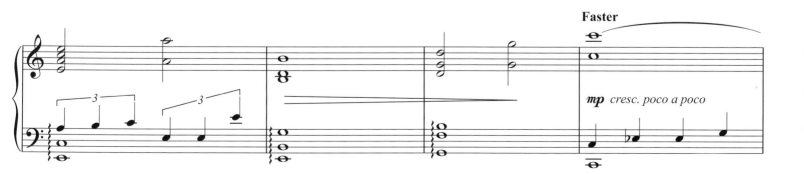

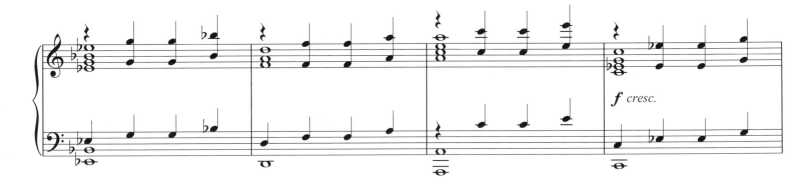

PUTTING THE MISS IN MISSION

from MISSION IMPOSSIBLE: GHOST PROTOCOL

Music by MICHAEL GIACCHINO

Slowly, expressively

Pedal ad lib. throughout

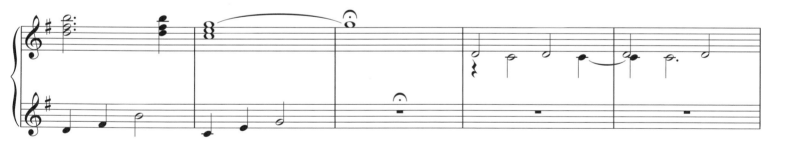

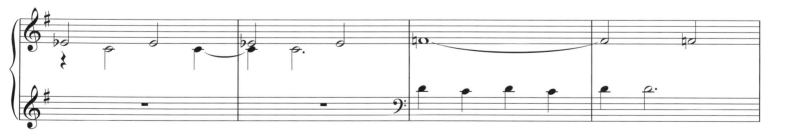

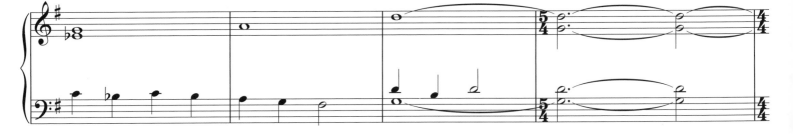

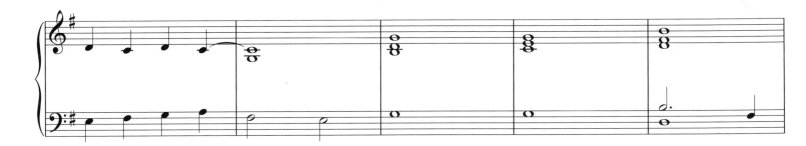

RATATOUILLE MAIN THEME
from RATATOUILLE

Music by MICHAEL GIACCHINO

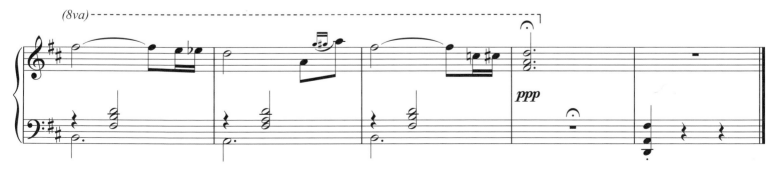

REBELLIONS ARE BUILT ON HOPE

from ROGUE ONE

Music by MICHAEL GIACCHINO

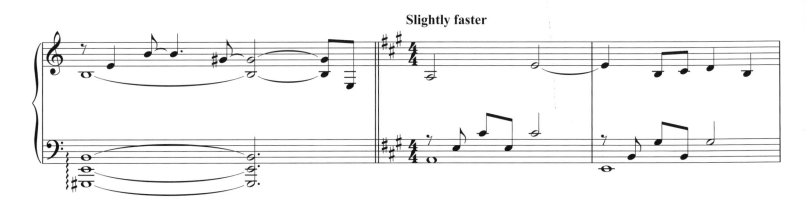

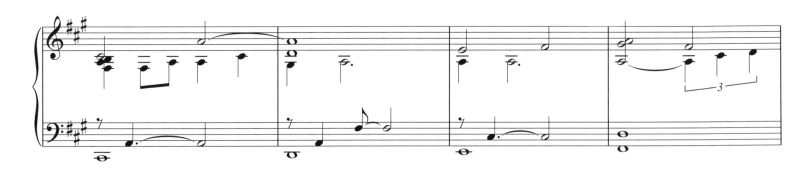

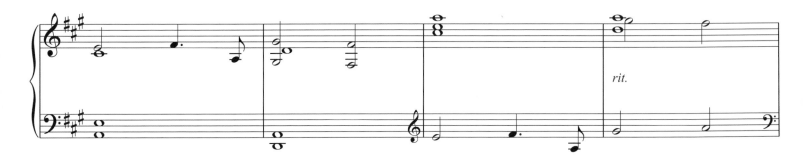

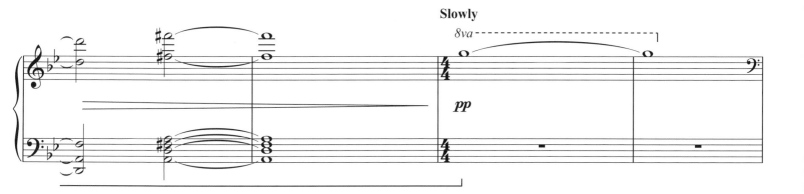

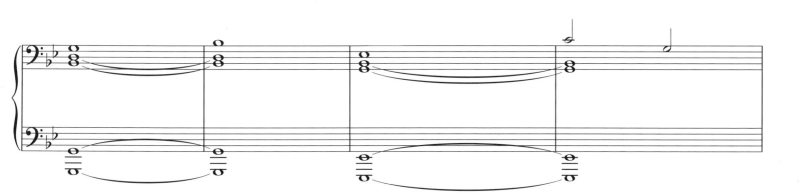

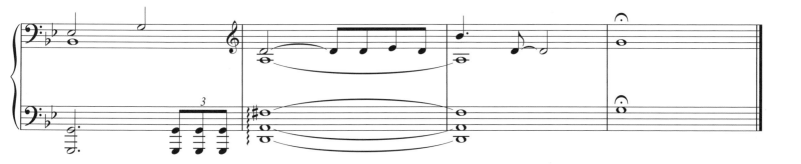

SONATA IN DARKNESS
from THE BATMAN

Music by MICHAEL GIACCHINO

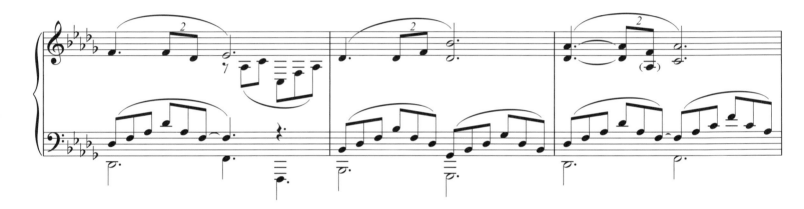

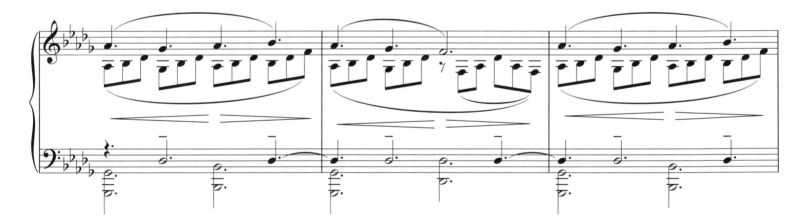

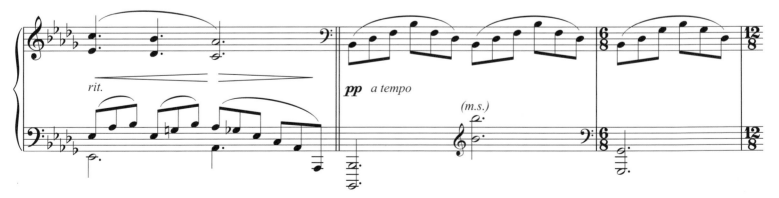

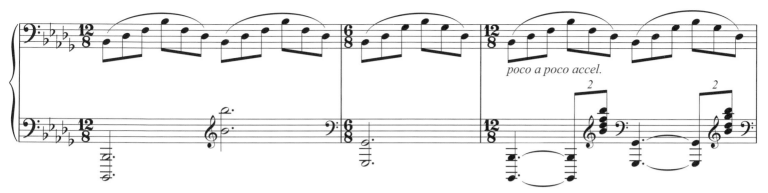

poco a poco accel.

Maestoso

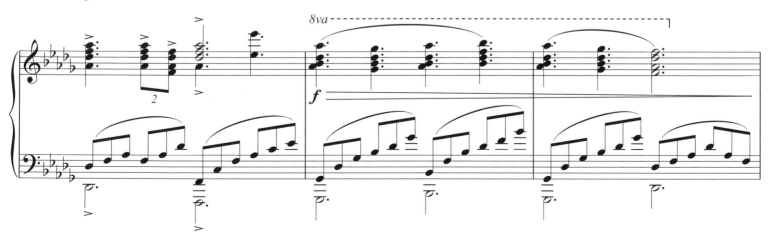

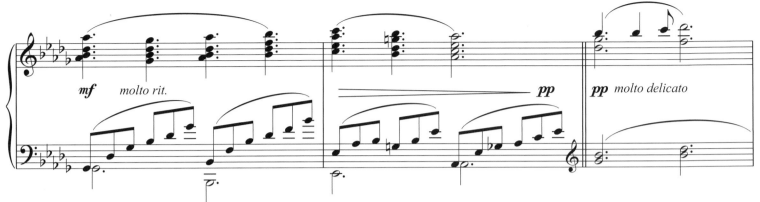

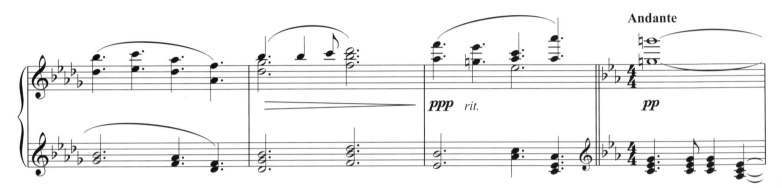

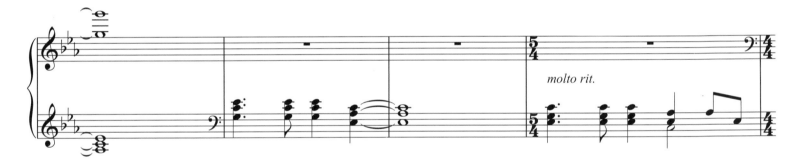

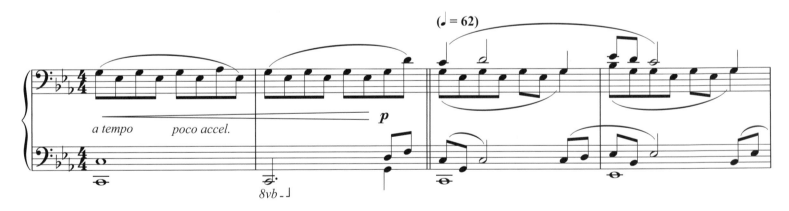

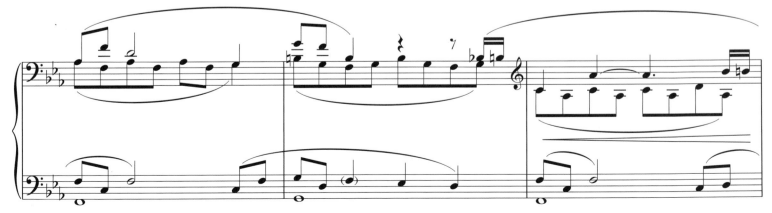

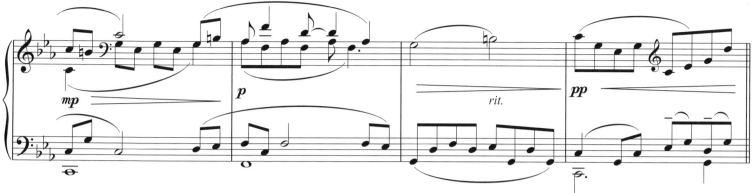

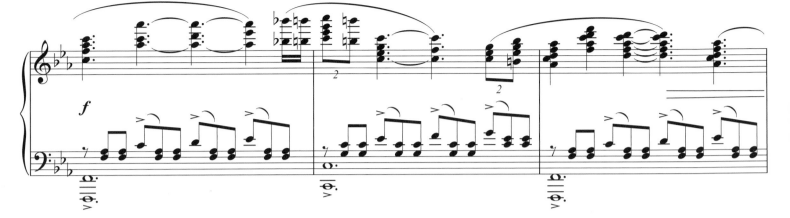

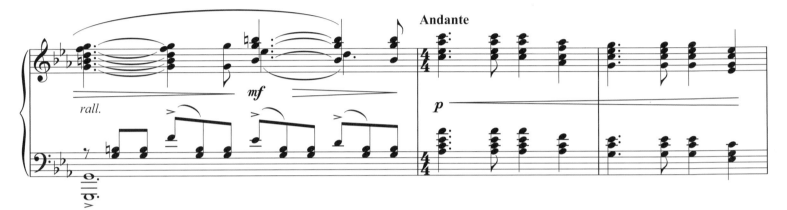

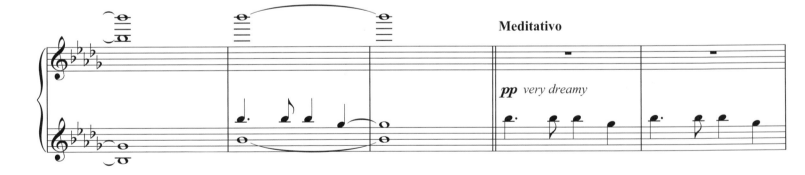

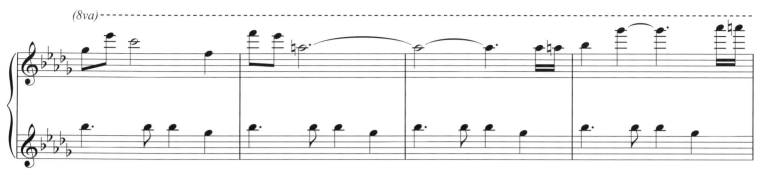

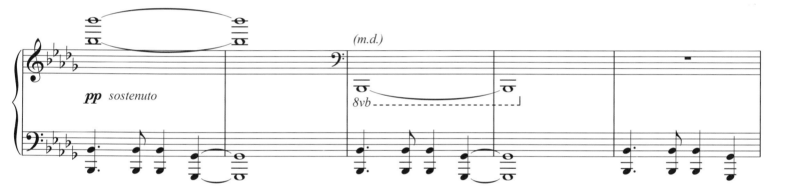

Con moto

Poco più mosso

Animando poco a poco

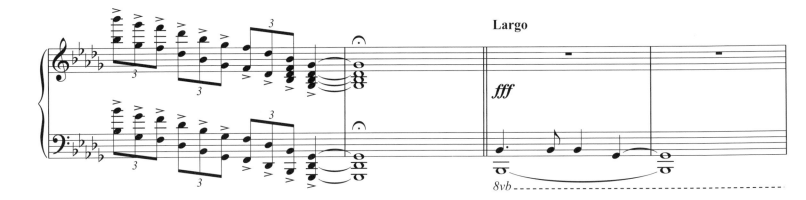

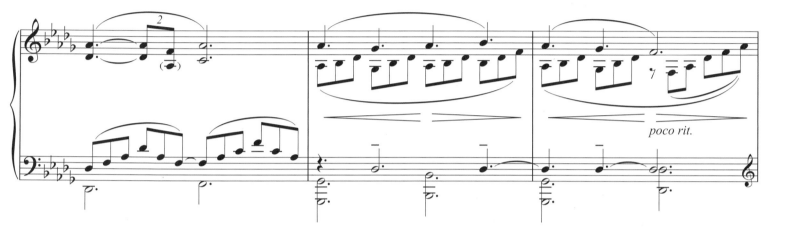

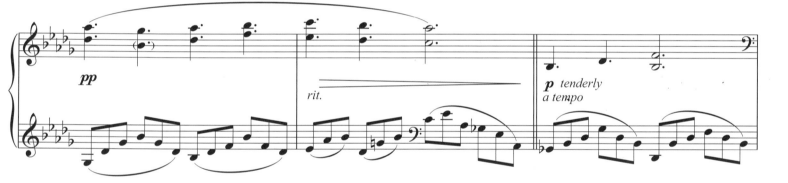

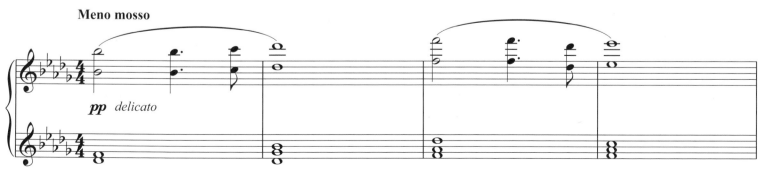

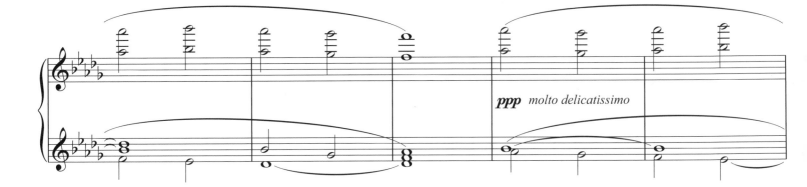

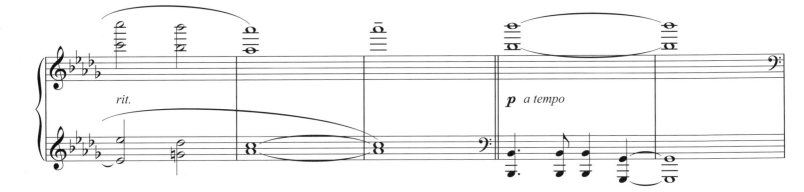

WEREWOLF BY NIGHT: MANE THEME

from WEREWOLF BY NIGHT

Music by MICHAEL GIACCHINO

Molto adagio, rubato

SPIDER-MAN: NO WAY HOME MAIN THEME

from SPIDER-MAN: NO WAY HOME

Music by MICHAEL GIACCHINO

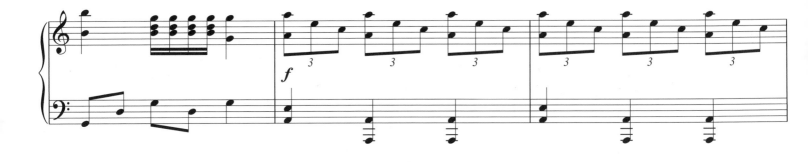

WE CAN STILL STOP HER

from INSIDE OUT

Music by MICHAEL GIACCHINO

Play 4 times

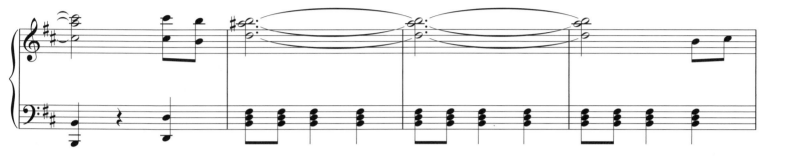

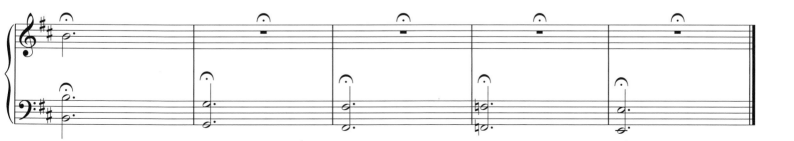

STAR TREK
from STAR TREK

Music by MICHAEL GIACCHINO

Moderately slow, in 2

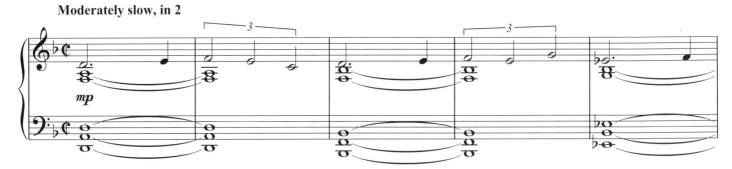

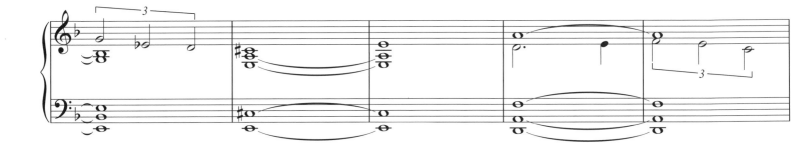

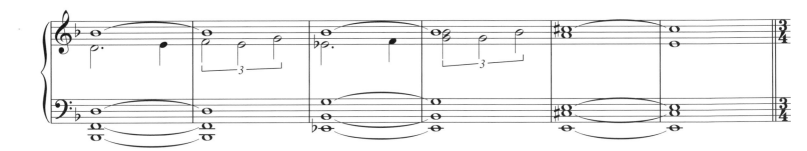

Faster